Wayfarer Of Thoughts

A collection of prose, quotations, and free verse

AFROZ

BookLeaf Publishing

Presentation by *BookLeaf Publishing*

Web: www.bookleafpub.com

E-mail: info@bookleafpub.com

ISBN: 978-93-5721-149-9

First edition 2023

To those folks with a youthful spirit who were always willing to broaden their horizons and grow.

One day when I chose to tell my tale, I ended up with a pen and paper, and it went like this.....

Haven't we all been hard on ourselves at some point in our lives?

At least once. Yes, sometimes for some reason and sometimes without any cause. Thus, it's all fine and so normal, isn't it? But why does it feel out of place at times? Especially when we cannot take it properly in a way that you can recover and be back to normal again. Isn't it a bit unfair to do that to ourselves? When we want to be the happiest at times, don't we deserve to vent out our frustrations, especially when everything is pushing us to be not fine? Yet, we don't choose to do that and pretend like nothing is bothering us when everything actually is. Is it only the trouble of accepting it, or do we lack the courage?

Isn't it inevitable to inquire about yourself and to be aware of things that are happening within you?

However, there will be circumstances in our lives when we feel like all of them carried on with their lives as they should, as you should as well, but you find yourself still not healed up and trying to escape from reality. You get to remember all your deeds from your past, which pops into your head constantly, and you get concerned about the little things that no longer make any sense. Even your life itself starts to highlight all those things. Gradually, you will know that everything changed and you no longer have authority over the things that have already happened. You cannot do anything other than make yourself feel secure and fine, and the reality hits harder than we think. From time to time, it's arduous because it takes a lot of courage to accept the change. Though your emotions will take a toll on you, in time, they will make you realise that to move on, you have to feel the pain; if you are not strong enough to have it, then you will never be strong enough to let it out. It's necessary to retain your energy, your strength, your playfulness, and your craziness to be you and to always be just you.

Because nothing changes when you hold on to your pent-up emotions, which only need to be let go.

Maybe sometimes it all feels like an unfulfilled dream, but it comes your way when you give yourself a chance to get enough of what you really want, and you will see yourself slightly changing in the process and getting along the track.

But when you adhere to the idea of perfection, it frequently feels exhausting and unpredictable. Yes, we all strive for perfection and often neglect to savour the seemingly little moments. Eventually, we realise that there is no such thing as "happily ever after." It's all about enjoying life, being present, and cherishing the memories. Only then is life worthwhile, or it's worthwhile to claim one is alive.

Thus, it's all about you and your life. To live, one must experience the ups and downs of the epic adventure that is life, where you occasionally feel hopeless and want to give up. However, it is understood that when life presents us with adversities, we cannot have good times, but they will make you aware that it's just a matter of getting better at dealing with them and surviving. After all, life is all about giving yourself a chance to smile every day rather than holding onto grudges, and thus, one day, you will open your eyes and get to know that life has come a long way.

How many years did it take you to finally understand who you are? Or are you just learning about it now?

However, I was unable to escape the fact that it took me 22 freaking years to accept myself completely. Now you will be wondering what led me to this sudden conclusion. It's not anything that big, but yes, I got hurt by some words that came from a complete stranger.

I probably shouldn't have given them that much weight. Yes, it was all about that, which caused me to reflect on the purpose of the past 22 years. It's been 22 years since I've been in this world and have I ever learned to know and comprehend myself in these 22 years?

Although I was having a very hard time getting this out of my head. How could I take those words and misunderstand myself? I shouldn't have done that. Is it possible that my lack of self-awareness is the reason why I took those words rather than choosing to ignore them?

On the other hand, life presented me with some other challenges in between. However, I wasn't bothered by it, and again, what about those words—am I supposed to match them fairly well? Surely not. What else is, then? Maybe it's my penance for not knowing myself for 22 years. I didn't even ask myself this until 22 years.

Am I too late to make sense of the situation? I'll say it again: I'm not sure. Some part of my consciousness was working so hard to convince myself that it was not me, that those words have nothing to do with me, and that they will never define me. But it doesn't seem to be having any effect on me; it's still there.

Does this 22-year-old want me to accept this?

Does this 22-year-old want me to carry those words?

Or what more does it want me to do?

How can one simple inquiry cause me this much distress and confusion?

Do these 22 years not seem like enough time for me to realise that we should not give importance to rubbish things?

Perhaps this "22" is simply a number and should not be taken into account. Maybe I'm still attempting to make sense of things. Maybe I still need to learn something after 22 years that I haven't yet. Again, I don't know; I suppose my desire for clarity led me to confront myself with the question, "Have you ever even tried to understand yourself?" I was speechless.

What does it mean to say that I am someone who deserves to be accepted and understood exactly as I am? It never goes well if I don't bring this to a close. But how long does it take me to convince myself that those words don't really matter, it's not me, and I don't owe anyone an explanation but myself for the inquiry that brought me to this conclusion:

"What have these 22 freaking years been for, if not for myself?"

Even if you knew me, would you comprehend?

Even if I don't want people to remember what they will remember after hearing my name, people will refer to me as a survivor. I simply detest being referred to as a rape victim; I prefer to be addressed solely by my identity rather than what I've gone through. Even though you know me, you don't know him as well as I do that 25-year-old. I recall our physical interactions, including his face, eyes, and hands—all of which I wish I could forget.

How could he do that to me if you are the one who made him in the same manner that you created me and everyone else, God?

Even if you know me, you won't recall this day as vividly as I do. December 12th. Winter was in full swing, my favourite season, but I had no idea that it would turn out to be a spooky night for which I didn't want to be remembered. I was pulled to the ground by someone while it was completely dark and the shutters were locked. I objected, but he grabbed me and started with my neck.

I kept saying no, no, no, but it seemed like I was pleading with a brick wall. Although he has large eyes, mercy cannot be seen in them. He brutally treated every inch of me, ripping my garments to pieces. It was so bloody painful that I couldn't forget it!

Even if you know me, you won't be able to understand what I felt. I was too afraid to even look at myself. For the very first time, I questioned the purpose of my existence. Was this my fate? What did I do to deserve to experience such destruction?

Even if you know me, you won't understand how he left. He left me in pieces like a ruthless butcher, shattering both my body and soul. He left with no regrets or worries. I could hardly move because of the blood stains all over my body, the tears that were streaming down my face, and the fact that my hands were resting on the ground. There was no one to whom I could run; there was just complete silence. For the first time ever, I detested it and was unable to find peace in it. I've never seen myself in this much pain.

Even if you knew me, you wouldn't know how desperately I begged him to let me go. I wanted to go home so much. I repeatedly begged and sobbed so hard, but nothing could get him to change his mind. I was unable to feel my body as well as myself; the pain was real. If you had chosen to let me go, I would have forgiven you, but in spite of all my pleading, you refused to do so. Now say, "Do you deserve forgiveness?" Do you qualify as a human? No, you weren't that; you were a wild, aggressive man who killed a 14-year-old girl who was a daughter, a sister, and more than that, a human being. Even if you know me, you won't be able to predict how I will ever move past this catastrophe. Do I get justice? Do I recover? Live or die? I don't know, but one thing is for certain: He will search for me and beg for my pardon one day.

He will panic and look for me the day he realises he will die mercilessly. But you won't recall my face, my name, or anything else about me; all you will recall is my voice, which represents my desperate desire to survive that day. When you hear that voice, you will realise how cruelly you treated me. Now, even after remembering all that you did to me, if you still search for me and think that you are deserving of forgiveness and mercy, may I ask you: where have all these things gone when I asked you?

Have you ever mentioned someone as a mistake in your life?

They are the reason for your helplessness and many sufferings. They were never someone whom you thought they would be, and there came that woman who was devoid of humane feelings and who wasn't good enough, not even a bit. you were not deserving to have met my friend. My friend thought you were too good to be true and too perfect to carry what that humble soul had for you,

but needless to say, you were cruel to it, lady! You left him in vain for having been there for you—for you, who deserved nothing, not even his company. He was too kind to you, lady. Are you remembering those days when things weren't as you expected and, when you ended up awful, and the only person left with you was him?

At times when you appeared to be aggressive and more vulnerable, he never thought to give you up and never questioned the need to have you in his life because he knew somewhere he couldn't do that. Though he was racked up in pain, he kept all this to himself, as elsewhere he knew his words wouldn't matter to whom they should.

In those days, towards your unpleasant deeds, he only said "it's okay," not because everything felt fine but because he hoped that one day everything would turn out as he wished. But needless to say, it was all just his evasion to survive, and those days were all about just surviving. He doesn't know how to be stronger than this. His tears were even meaningless in your cruel world, but you women did not deserve to meet him, and I have no idea what drew him to you. I asked him about it. He didn't say anything, but I could see through his eyes. Hey, lady, he knew it all. He knew he wasn't deserving of these inhuman acts of cruelty that he tolerated. He was mindless enough to think you were too good.

He was in your unmerciful place with his desperate mind. He carried an ocean of suffering. No more amends or explanations could make him find peace within himself because he took all the pain he could and walked all the way you made him. What more can you ask from a person? Despite knowing how much you meant to him and how cruel you made him feel, you women disgraced yourselves by refusing to let him go and instead forcing him to stay.

Wasn't this a sad place?

Weren't you a pitiful being?

Was it all enough for you?

I hope so. If not, where will you take all your sins to? You won't find a place because you already filled that place with much disgrace, which could have accepted all your apologies with ease.

However, now he only has his unspeakable tragedy for you. You only left that to him.

He was the one you could always rely on and whom you could walk with throughout your life. He was more than you could ever get or ask for. But you, women, you're bad. You won't get much of him by now, and where are your mere words that you always make up? Now say those words were all lies that will be revealed over time, and thus you were always good at making him swallow falsehood. What's worse than that? It is unfortunate that he chose the wrong person to fall in love with. I can see him taking his frustrations and reminding himself that it was all just a moment of love that left him with a scar that is never going to show he survived. He was lost in your bittersweet words, which had already formed a locus in his heart and caused him to travel far in the hope of those lies, which he had neither forgotten nor forgiven. Wailing in sorrow, he only wished he had ever gotten a chance to rewrite his fate.

Now don't bruise him anymore. I hope you had enough to be content and fulfilled. Just leave silently. Let me help my friend find the courage to rectify his mistake.

Let him heal, and let your longing to wound him rest and not be revived.

Let him heal.

"Though life doesn't have a clear vision for everything, still we could spell the word Destiny and walk into the miracle of life with a past which made you realize and accept this."

"A camera which holds nice pictures in it, sometimes doesn't have those sweet memories which we could only capture so beautifully like nothing else."

"You cannot change people's perceptions of you;
you just get better at dealing with them."

"It is better to let go of the past than to hold onto something that has already come to an end, especially if it makes you feel pessimistic about the future."

"It's not about saying grandiose things or thinking like a philosopher, it's all about what you truly feel on the inside, it's all that matters."

"Despite the fact that we live shorter lives, happiness is not the only thing that determines if life is meaningful. We only live when we believe that the lives we are leading are worthwhile, regardless of how happy they may be."

"Keep in mind that never lose sight of the things that helped you see your own value, if you do, it maybe quite challenging to get it back."

"Accept what you feel right and pursue what you had accepted."

"Everybody will not be with you every time, you have got to acknowledge that before you accept anybody in your life."

‘expectation’; it was all just a lie when I looked back.

"Even if you face criticism, it won't matter if you know who you are, what you believe and what you are doing, then, you won't feel the need to defend yourself."

"Nothing is more or less until you value it in your own way."

"Perhaps it seems difficult for you, but it appears to be simple for someone else, and this is what makes all the difference."

"Replacing things with a later valuation is fine, though it may not always be possible to get them back but you will learn the right lesson that will stay with you for the rest of your life and that cannot be replaced."

"Ignoring absurdity is the wisest course of action."

"It's not worth holding onto something that drains you, even if it meets your needs."

"That said, fate may not always live up to your expectations but why not give it a shot when the unpredictability of life presents a chance for possibility."

"There are times when we awaken and fail to remember that we do have a life, a day to live, the chance to discover new things, get new insights and embrace both joy and sorrow, there are times when we fail to appreciate the blessing that each minute of our lives is."

"You should be able to ignore it if someone is able to insult you."

"Even though you may have a lot of passions, there may be times when life only permits you to pursue one of them, despite this, your other interests are still meaningful, but in the end, it all comes down to giving you what you deserve in the greatest way possible, and that's a wonderful thing."

“In the end, living is all about choosing to smile every day over harboring resentments.”

"Sometimes words don't have the power to conclude some situations."

"There is no better time to speak anything than when you are experiencing it as true, if you have something to say but have been holding it back, go ahead and say it now rather than waiting for the appropriate moment, maybe those words might just change your life."

“If you want the most excellent reply, inquire yourself.”

"Chomp your sentiments, feel the torment and walk it off."

"Despite my many great efforts, I continue to feel unsatisfied. It's alright, my motivation to do better everyday, in my opinion, comes from this."

"Don't lose yourself in the process of trying to get adapted and adjusted."

"A dream is pointless unless you have a reason to continuously work for it."

"Set yourself free to be felt and to experience the many shades of existence."

"When all is said and done, if you feel that the only thing left for you is yourself, love yourself since you are the only one who has experienced and felt all these things."

"Do not just always bother your possessions, also disturb your abilities."

“Everyone has flaws, but the best version of oneself to become is the one that acknowledges their flaws while continuing to have faith in themselves and strive to achieve greatness.”

"It's not that you don't love something, it's just that some things are meant to be given up since holding onto them only makes the pain worse."

"When we pretend to be nice to someone in order to gain our needs, we are not being good; we are simply prioritizing."

"Some truths are better left unspoken to not let you shattered."

"In the course of trying to understand who you are, you'll also discover and pick up new skills."

"It's not about what we know, more than that, it's all about accepting what we know."

"Maybe a lie could spare you from the storm but not from your fate."

" Decide who deserves your words and who doesn't, with those who don't, it's better to remain silent because some people only deserve silence."

“I am no more a storm, I turned into a scar which speaks, which is powerful more than a thousand verses.”

"Learn to say goodbye to the things that are not good for you."

"You will find the best way if you are aware of both the wrong and right ways to do anything."

"Learn to be close to others while yet maintaining your standards and boundaries."

"Cherish every moment to make your memories last a lifetime."

"Feed your attention to the reason behind your goal, but if that reason is illogical, turn away."

"Don't invest yourself too much in anything without a good reason because that ' anything ' is too big for you to invest in."

"Don't make commitments unless you have faith in yourself."

"The most beautiful thing and the kindest thing about you are both inside you, you don't need to look for it, all you want is to just treasure it."

I don't

But sometimes I do give love to the people who actually don't deserve it.

But I forgive and I forgive, until they kill me with their words, but still a single drop of water doesn't roll down from my eyes because, it's my obstinacy and thus, you cannot explain my situation with no more words. I am not fed up or obsessed, but I am not also empty, as I don't want to prove to anyone how strong I was in that situation.

It brings to mind a monsoon day whenever I am having one of those bad days.
The sky was cloudy and it was pouring heavily.
I was only aware that I needed to get through the fog somehow.
Like everyone else, I was carrying my umbrella and moving forth with an extremely-sourced sense of optimism.
With a smile on my face, I strolled around like a carefree bird.
I then had the feeling that the situation was perfect for me at that precise moment,
As much as it makes me smile now,
I am still left to question how wonderful that moment was ever.

The words got stuck in my mind,
The verses got confused in my heart and
My whole thoughts seem to be mixed before
writing the poem.
But, after writing the poem, it feels stuck in the
heart of readers like the way it got stuck in my
mind.
Thus, it all feels done the way it should be
understood between readers and the poet.

A part of him was contended and grateful for that one occurrence that left a considerable impact on him once,

As time went on, that joy was gently turning into grief, for which each part of his soul was now regretting for witnessing that incident because he came to know that the hope which he was getting through it was nothing but falsehood.

He was crammed with lies that once showered him with a pure sense of ecstasy and hope and thus, left him hopeless too.

That's how life chooses to reveal the truth and time choose to make a huge difference in your thoughts and emotions and now you can see how this 'falsehood' is going to entangle him with misery and leave him with absolutely nothing but a pain to carry.

Are you sure?
Are you sure that you will be back at the same place?
Are you sure that you will be back with the same people?
Are you sure that you will be back with the same feeling?
Are you sure that you will be back with the same kind of vibe?
Are you sure?

If not, one day you will wake up and you will only feel all those moments like a dream that you could wish for once more, and you will realise that you never lived those moments and you will never be able to live them again. Until then you only have this moment while it lasts, and you may choose to either miss it or live it.

Something left him fearful

Something left him unsatisfied

Something left him wild

Something left him dishonest

Something left him rude

Something left him unlovable

Something left him in pain

Something left him feeling guilty

Something left him in the dark

Something left him too hard to rewrite that

Something to someone; his soul didn't find the courage to embrace it.

Yet, he knew the truth but it wasn't enough.

I occasionally want to write about something.
What is it about art?
What it is about colours
A characteristic of nature
Some aspect of night
A thing regarding days
Something about the world as it is
Also anything about life

But each time I try something, I find myself being held back by the same thought: am I too knowledgeable to write about it? If not, what do other people think about it?

And even thinking about it was a huge mistake. It doesn't matter your level of experience, pick up a pen and paper and start writing about how you are feeling. Put your all into it just the way you like it; it won't matter because others didn't feel the same way you did when writing about it.

Through writing, I hope to fully express myself.
The paper and the pen were there to capture each
and every tears that fell from my eyes.
At times, I feel quite depressed because there are
moments when I can't even write a word.
I made an attempt to swallow some
My chaotic mind, trembling hands, and all of my
efforts will suddenly be a fuss for the paper.
Now, I tried my hardest, I gave it everything I had
and I just did it.
My fear has vanished into the depths of the night
and now I am content with myself